IT'S OK TO SAY NO

A Book for Parents and Children to Read Together

Written by
Amy C. Bahr

Illustrated by
Frederick
Bennett Green

GROSSET & DUNLAP

Copyright © 1986 by RGA Publishing Group, Inc. and Frederick Bennett Green. Concept by
RGA Publishing Group, Inc. IT'S OK TO SAY NO is a trademark of RGA Publishing Group, Inc.
Published by Grosset & Dunlap, a member of The Putnam Publishing Group, New York.
Printed in Italy. Published simultaneously in Canada. Library of Congress Catalog
Card Number: 85-080573 ISBN 0-448-15328-9 A B C D E F G H I J

NOTE TO PARENTS

As responsible parents, we protect our children by teaching them the rules and regulations of water safety, fire safety, and bicycle safety. The IT'S OK TO SAY NO Picture Books will help you teach your child the most important safety lesson of all—body safety.

As you read this book with your child, or with a child you care about, you may want to expand on some of the situations, or you may prefer to read the simple text just as it is. In either case, this book should stimulate discussion. It's important that you take the time to let your child respond to questions asked in the book, and that you listen to any questions the child may have. If you feel awkward or embarrassed, you should direct these questions to someone you and your child feel comfortable with. Above all, the child must understand and remember the rules that will help him or her to recognize and respond to threatening situations.

The IT'S OK TO SAY NO Picture Books are not meant to scare but rather to educate. Children need to learn the words and phrases in the books and use them to say no, to tell their parents if something is wrong, and to avoid dangerous situations. Adults, in turn, must learn to listen and must give their children the freedom to tell.

—The Children's Justice Foundation, Inc.

When you're a kid, lots of people tell you what to do. Your dad tells you to be home by dinnertime, and you say, "OK, Dad."

Your teacher tells you to finish a page in your workbook, and you say, "Yes, Ms. Smith."

When your coach tells you to put away the balls, you say, "Sure, Coach."

Even if it's something you don't want to do, like taking out the trash for your mom, you usually say, "Oh, all right," and do it anyway.

But sometimes it's OK to say no to an adult, especially when your parents aren't around. What should you say if you're walking home and a stranger wants you to talk to him?

You should say no. Run home and tell your mom and dad.

What would you say if someone offers to buy you a present?

Even if you want it, say no. Don't take anything from anyone unless your mom or dad is with you.

What should you say if a teenager you don't know says, "Hop on! I'll give you a ride"?

You should say no and walk away, even if you want a ride.
Never go anywhere, even just down your own street, without
telling your parents or babysitter where you'll be.

If a neighbor asks you to come into her garage and see the new kittens, you should say...

"I'll have to go ask my mom first."

What should you say if someone you don't know asks to take your picture?

You should say no and run home.

What should you say if someone offers you a dollar to help him find his lost puppy?

You should say no. Run home and tell your mom or dad. Adults ask other adults for help.

What should you do if you're at the movies with a friend and someone touches you and makes you feel uncomfortable?

You should say, "Stop it!" very loudly. Get up and tell the manager of the theater, then sit down in a different seat.

If a friend of your dad's talks to you about touching and kissing and makes you feel yucky, it's OK to say no or walk away. Talk to your dad about what happened.

It's OK to say no if anyone tries to touch the private parts of your body. Your private parts are the places that are covered by your bathing suit.

Your body belongs to you, and you have the right to say who touches it. It's OK to say no and run away if someone is making you feel weird or uncomfortable.

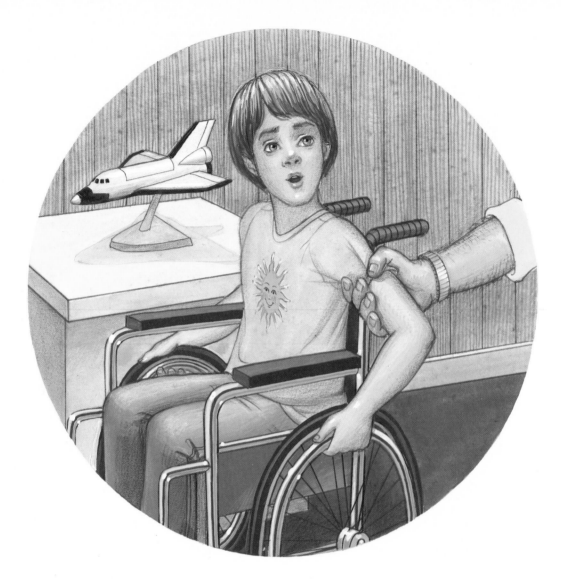

It's **OK** to say no if someone grabs you and won't let go—even if it's just a game.

It's OK to say no—even to someone you love.

It's OK to say no—even if you said yes last time.

If you have a yucky feeling about any situation, it's OK to say no and run away. And if anything happens that makes you feel confused or scared, it's OK to talk about it with your mom or dad or with the person who reads you this book.

Now you know that sometimes it's OK to say no!